Black Boy Shining!
ABCs of Character and Spirit

by Rhonda Bryant

Illustrated by Stacy Hummel

Black Boy Shining! ABCs of Character and Spirit
Text copyright © 2019 Rhonda Bryant
Illustrations copyright © 2019 Stacy Hummel
Edited by Ti Kendrick Hall

All rights reserved. Printed in the United States of America.
No part of this book may be used or reproduced in any manner whatsoever without written permission, except in the case of brief quotations embedded in critical articles and reviews.

For more information, contact:
info@themoriahgroup.com

www.rhondabryantedd.com/blackchildshining

Library of Congress Control Number: 2019915323
ISBN: 978-1-7341118-2-8

First Edition

This book is dedicated to Andrew, my first-born. You changed my life in amazing ways and are a true inspiration. I love you!

A stands for **AMBITIOUS.**
Big goals I will achieve!
I set my sights high for my life;
I only must believe.

B says, "I AM BOLD."
I'm not scared to speak out.
I have so many big ideas
I'd love to tell you about!

C means I am **CONFIDENT**.
I walk with my head high.
I have greatness growing inside of me
that nobody can deny.

D proclaims, **"I AM DILIGENT."**
I do my best each day.
I stick to tasks and see them through!
Excellence is my way.

E means I'm **EAGER.**
I'm thrilled to learn so much!
From planes up high to ants down low,
I've got a world to see and touch!

F says, "I AM FRIENDLY."
I smile at everyone I meet.
I'm kind to all my friends at school
and the new kid down the street.

G stands for **GIFTED!**
I am capable and smart.
When I grow up, I could cure disease
or make beautiful art.

H means I am **HOPEFUL.**
I see beyond what's here.
I dream of a world filled with love
for people far and near.

I – Yes, I'm **INTELLIGENT!**
I'm as smart as I can be!
My favorite phrase is, "Did you know?"
I'm full of fun facts, you see.

J – Oh, I am **JOYFUL!**
I'm happy from the inside out.
Ice cream truck treats and laughing with friends,
sweet moments make my heart shout!

K says, "I AM KINGLY."
I know my history.
From Mansa Musa to Shaka Zulu,
I am their legacy!

L stands for **LIVELY!**
No dull moments with me!
I could jump and play and wrestle all day.
It's so much fun, you see!

M means I am **MIGHTY;**
so very strong and brave.
Even when things are sometimes hard,
courageous is how I behave.

N says, "I AM NOBLE."
Strong morals are a must.
I am honest, courteous, and have love for all.
I truly try to be just.

Oh yes, I'm **ORIGINAL!**
There is no one quite like me!
From my quick wit to this handsome face —
there can't be another me!

P means I am **PLAYFUL**.
I just love to have some fun.
Pretending I'm in outer space
or dancing in the sun.

Q says, "I am QUIET sometimes."
I take a moment to rest.
I think on all the things I've learned
and plan what to do next.

R means I am **RADIANT.**
I have a special glow.
I'm joy and light from the inside out
and I spread it wherever I go.

S says, **"I AM SACRED."**
A precious child of this season.
My spirit, my love, my being is special.
I am on this earth for a reason.

T stands tall for **TRUSTWORTHY.**
My promises I keep.
To clean my room or feed the dog
and not leave my clothes in a heap.

U means I'm **UNSELFISH.**
It feels so good to share.
Then, we can all have fun
and it shows how much I care.

V says, "I AM VALIANT."
Determined, and strong, too.
I stand tall for what is right
for both me and you!

W means I'm **WONDERFUL.**
In my Blackness, I am proud.
My brown skin is a precious creation.
Black boy shining! Say it loud!

X — Oh, I'm **EXPRESSIVE**
I say what needs to be said.
Happy, sad, excited, or scared—
I speak what's in my head.

Y says, "I AM YOUNG."
Life goals, I have a slew!
I'll dream big and shoot for the stars.
I wonder what I'll do?

Z exclaims, **"I'M ZEALOUS!"**
I'm as excited as can be.
Learning new and interesting things
is a great experience for me!

I'm a Black Boy Shining!
I am:

- **A**mbitious
- **B**old
- **C**onfident
- **D**iligent
- **E**ager
- **F**riendly
- **G**ifted
- **H**opeful
- **I**ntelligent
- **J**oyful
- **K**ingly
- **L**ively
- **M**ighty
- **N**oble
- **O**riginal
- **P**layful
- **Q**uiet
- **R**adiant
- **S**acred
- **T**rustworthy
- **U**nselfish
- **V**aliant
- **W**onderful
- e**X**pressive
- **Y**oung
- **Z**ealous

The End

About the Author

Rhonda Tsoi-A-Fatt Bryant, EdD is a researcher, educator, and advocate in youth development. She has dedicated her career to improving the lives of youth who are marginalized all over the world. She has two children—Andrew and Leigha—who are the inspiration for her children's books. With this book, Dr. Bryant seeks to shower young boys with love and affirmation to carry in their hearts for the rest their lives.

Credit: Breana Isbell Photography

CPSIA information can be obtained
at www.ICGtesting.com
Printed in the USA
BVHW021158170120
569685BV00005B/1